LEARN WITH TUNES

A Melodic Approach to the Violin for Individual or Class Instruction

by CARL GRISSEN

ISBN 978-1-70519-862-9

WILLIS MUSIC

EXCLUSIVELY DISTRIBUTED BY

HAL•LEONARD®

Visit Hal Leonard Online at
www.halleonard.com

World headquarters, contact:
Hal Leonard
7777 West Bluemound Road
Milwaukee, WI 53213
Email: info@halleonard.com

In Europe, contact:
Hal Leonard Europe Limited
1 Red Place
London, W1K 6PL
Email: info@halleonardeurope.com

In Australia, contact:
Hal Leonard Australia Pty. Ltd.
4 Lentara Court
Cheltenham, Victoria, 3192 Australia
Email: info@halleonard.com.au

PREFACE

To the Teacher

If the following suggestions are followed a short time before the pupil begins the study of the third position, the task of learning a new position will be greatly simplified.

The logical approach to the new position is through the tonal sense, the ear, not by struggling with notes.

The first finger tone is the most important in beginning a new position; if the student can place this tone with reasonable certainty, those that follow will be easy.

Without music, the teacher may tell the student that he is soon going into the third position, four new tones on each string. Then show him how to find the first finger tone on each string.

Use the string that is best adapted to the voice range of the pupil.

Ask the student to sing Sol, Do, a few times, telling him that Sol is the open string, and Do is the first finger tone on the D string.

With the hand in the third position the student plays Sol, Do:

Retaining the violin with chin and shoulder, the student should lower the left hand, and with the proper hand position find the tone several times to coördinate the tonal sense with the tactile.

Proceed in the same manner on each string, pointing out how each of the first finger tones is directly opposite one to the other.

Five minutes are enough for this preliminary approach; at the next lesson the student should be able to play Sol, Do in tune on each string with the first contact of the finger to the string.

At the next lesson period the procedure should be varied slightly to impart the idea of shifting between the first and the third positions.

By the time the review of fundamentals in the first position is completed, the pupil is prepared to play from notes in the third position with considerable assurance.

Carl Gruen

A REVIEW OF FUNDAMENTALS
In the First Position

Embellishments, the Half Position, Springing Bow

The Trill

A trill is to be played when the sign (*tr*) is placed above a note. This note is called the principal note. While the principal note is held down with one finger, the trilling finger plays the next note above, either a half or a whole tone, in rapid succession.

1. A slower, even trill is more effective than a trill that is uneven and unrhythmical.

2. The trill is as long as the value of the principal note.

3. An electrical bell gives a good idea of a fast, rhythmic trill.

4. Practice slowly and evenly at first, with the trilling finger close to the string, speed and control will come later.

5. Try to control the number of pulsations in each beat. Except for the initial attack, the trill is mostly without accentuation. The preparatory studies are accented to help control the number of pulsations to the beat.

6. In slow tempo more notes can be trilled to a beat than in a fast tempo.

Preparatory Exercise for the Trill

Play the four groups in each measure evenly, in strict time.

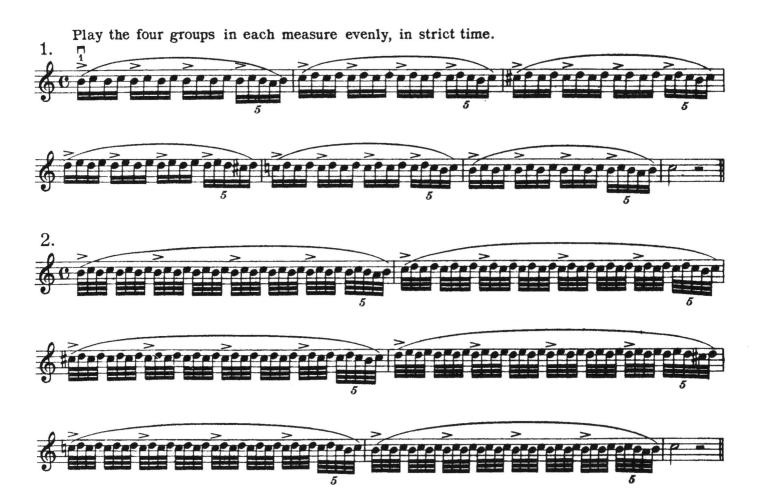

3. (a) The trill in fast tempo   (b) The trill in slow tempo

4. (a) In fast tempo   (b) In slow tempo

5. Practice in medium and slow tempo according to (a) and (b) in No. 3

6. Apply (a) and (b) of No. 4 to these trills

Grace Notes

The short appoggiatura (♪) has a dash through the stem of the
note, has no time value, and should be played lightly and delicately.
A mere flick of the finger is sufficient.

Short appog.   Double appog.

7.

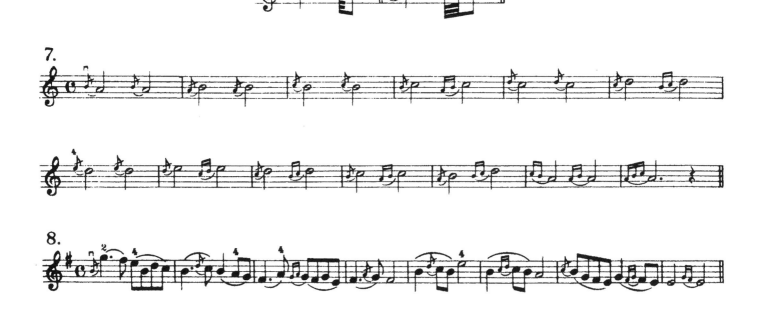

8.

The long appoggiatura (♪ or ♩) without a dash through the note stem, receives one half the value of an undotted note, two thirds the value of dotted notes.

1. The long appoggiatura as written

as played

2.

The mordent (𝄍) is an abbreviation of two notes that precede the principal note.

3.

The Turn

The turn (∾) is an abbreviation of four notes that follow the principal note.
The time value of the turn is taken from the principal note.
Most turns begin with the next note above the principal note.

A single note with the turn sign above, becomes a complete turn.

Placed to the right of an undotted note, the turn receives one half the value of the principal note.

4.

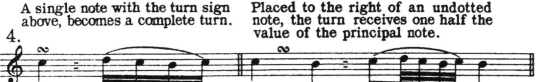

Placed after a dotted note, the turn takes on a triplet form, its last note being of equal value with the shorter note following the dotted principal note.

5. Evolution of the turn following a dotted note.

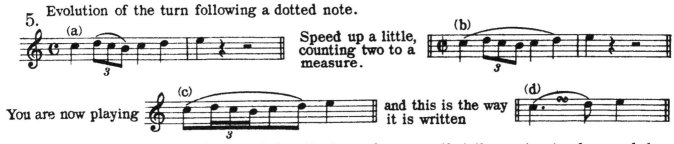

(a)

Speed up a little, counting two to a measure.

(b)

You are now playing

(c)

and this is the way it is written

(d)

Flats, sharps or naturals above or below the turn sign mean that the next note above or below the principal note is to be flatted or sharped accordingly.

Floridia

6.

The Half Position

The half position provides a convenient fingering for passages in the keys of four, five and six **sharps.** Each finger plays a half or a whole tone lower than in the first position.

This passage is awkward in the first position (a), but easy in the half position (b).

1.

2.

A Lonely Vigil

3.

Sentimental Mood

4. Before playing, recite the half position fingering for each note.

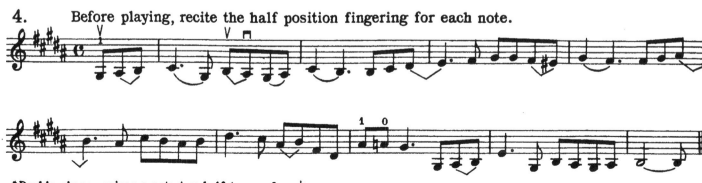

*Double sharp – raises a note two half tones: f✕ = g♮.

EVENING IN ALGIERS
The practical application of embellishments

The Muezzin's Call to Prayer

C.G.

Arabian Dance

The Springing Bow

In this type of bowing, the bow-stick should be held straight above the bow-hair. Use the middle of the bow with relaxed hand and a free wrist, the fourth finger entirely non-active. There is scarcely any lateral motion, but more of a vertical, automatic springing effect.

The Rain

A study in springing bow

LESSON 1

The Third Position

The notation of the Third Position as shown in the diagram and on the staff is to be memorized. In two weeks the pupil should be able to answer the following quiz:

Name the 1st finger notes in the third position starting from the E string; the 3rd finger notes starting from the G string; the 4th finger notes from the E string. Name the tone played by the 3rd finger on the D string? Name the 4th finger tone on the G string? etc.

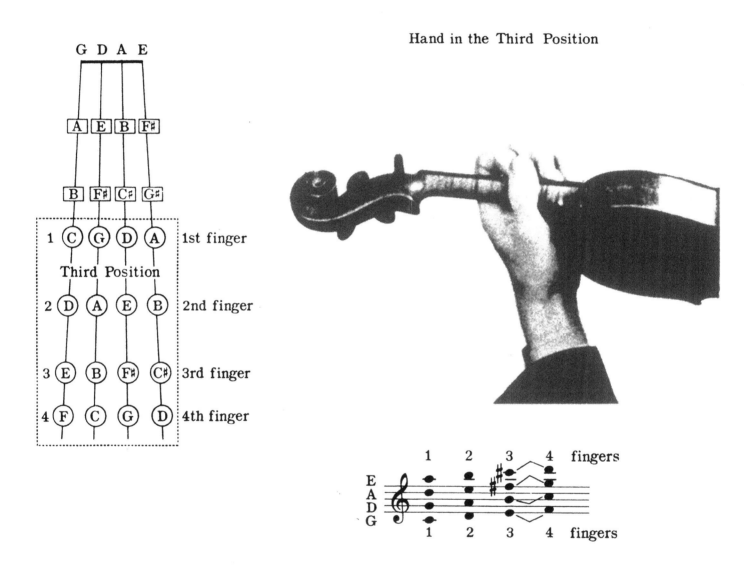

Hand in the Third Position

1. Maintain the same straight hand position in the Third as in the First Position.
2. The movement of the hand must start from the elbow with the thumb moving smoothly along the violin neck.
3. Do not shove the fingers forward before moving the hand and the thumb when shifting from the first to the third position.
4. Keep the first finger down as much as possible.

The A String

Roman numerals designate the position

March time

The E String

To gain sureness with the 1st finger often test with open string below.

LESSON 2
The Third Position
The A and E strings combined

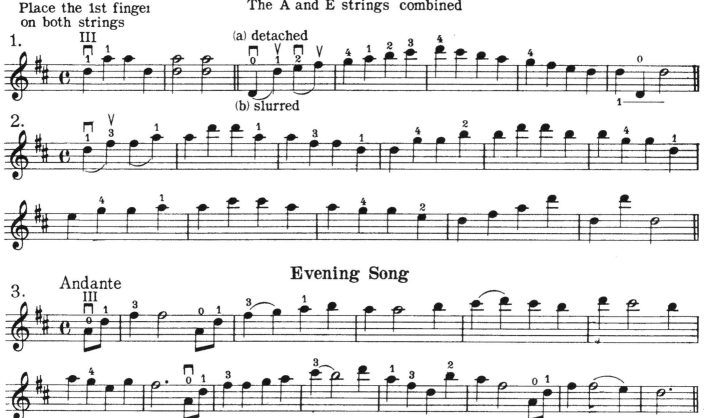

Place the 1st finger on both strings

1.

(a) detached

(b) slurred

2.

Evening Song

3. Andante

When beginning with the 2nd, 3rd or 4th finger, measure off these tones from the 1st finger. No. 4 begins with the 3rd, followed by the 2nd and 1st fingers. Place them in reverse order.

Believe Me If All Those Endearing Young Charms

Andantino

Irish Melody

4. Pupil

Alternate pupils on 1st and 2nd parts for intonation

Pupil

Teacher

LESSON 3
The Third Position
The D String

The Bass Drum

Play the open G string along with the upper notes.

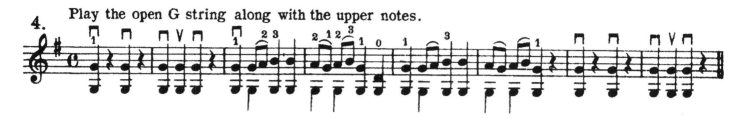

The D and A strings

Place the 1st finger on both strings

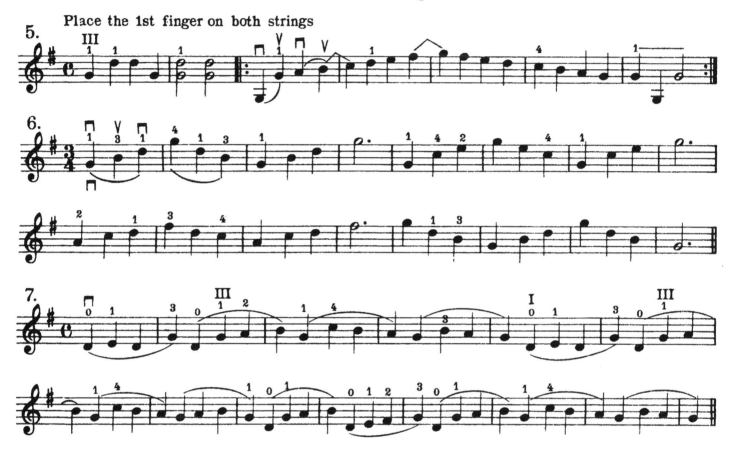

The Blacksmith and the Anvil

Keep the 1st finger down throughout

C.G.

LESSON 4
The Third Position

The G String

In Pensive Mood

C. G.

Valentine Day

C. G.

LESSON 5
The Third Position

The open string and the first finger shift between the first and third positions.

Look for the essentials in any study; in this etude the notes in the dotted brackets are important—give them extra attention—the others merely fill in.

The Huntsman's Song

C.G.

Allegretto

dim. e rit.

LESSON 6

Chromatic Progressions in the Third Position

Unequal 5ths in C major

B on the D string is a half tone higher than F on the A string

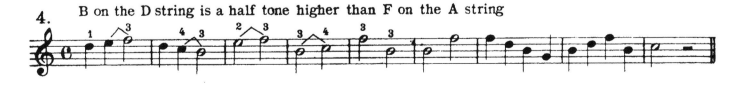

Youthful Spirits

LESSON 7

Shifting with one finger between the first and third positions

1. Give each note its full value before shifting.
2. Hold the violin firmly with the chin and the shoulder so that the left hand is free in the change of position.
3. Keep the shifting finger on the string between positions, relaxing finger pressure during the shift.
4. Use more bow on the first of two slurred notes.
5. Keep the hand straight and the thumb relaxed.
6. Avoid any whining sound in shifting, due to dragging the finger too heavily and slowly along the string.

Over Hill and Dale

Don't move the hand – stretch the
1st finger back a half tone

LESSON 8
The Portamento

When a finger glides up or down a string to make a smooth connection between the tones in different positions, the effect is called *portamento*.

1. The portamento between tones is, in most instances, only faintly audible.
2. Sing the second measure of "Old Folks at Home"; the sound of the voice between the syllables Swa-nee and Riv-er is the natural effect of portamento.
3. If a pupil has trouble with his intonation in shifting, play the position changes on the A, D and G strings in the first position, then with the fingering as given.
4. With detached notes the change of position must be timed exactly with the change of bow. In No. 3, fifth measure, the second finger leaves its note at the instant the up bow is changed to the down stroke.
5. The notes in parentheses, showing how far to slide the finger, are not to be heard.

Rigadoon

LESSON 9
Alternating the First and Third Positions

Chromatic progressions—accidentals

Cross Country

C. G.

The Bard's Story

C. G.

LESSON 10

Half and whole tone shifts in the first and third positions

3.

The Coquette

C.G.

4. Allegretto

Substitution Waltz

Changing positions by Substituting a different finger for the same tone

5.

LESSON·11
Harmonics

By extending the fourth finger from the third to the fourth position, the harmonic or over-tone on the octave from the open string will be found. These bell-like tones are used constantly in violin playing.

1. Do not press the string in playing harmonics, touch the string with the tip of the finger with feathery lightness.
2. The harmonics on each string are exactly opposite each other, and are indicated by the sign (o) placed above the note.

Pastoral

LESSON 12

The shift across strings between the first and third positions

Gavotte

Czardas

LESSON 13

The Second Position

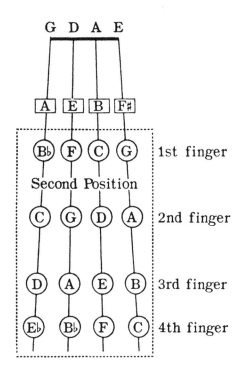

Memorize the fingering of the second position so that any note and finger can be identified without hesitation when the teacher begins the second position quiz.

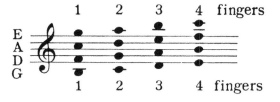

Hand in the Second Position

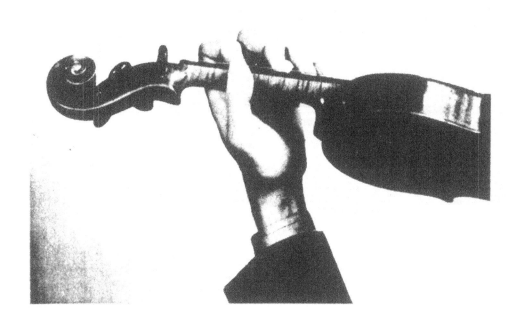

1. In shifting from the first to the second position, the shifting finger moves either a half or a whole tone; this calls for very little movement of the hand.
2. Maintain the straight hand position, moving the thumb along with the hand.
3. For good intonation keep the first finger on the strings as much as possible.
4. Remember there are only three possible movements of a finger when crossing from one string to another: (1) straight across; (2) down a half step; (3) up a half step—according to the unequal fifths in various keys.

Loch Lomond

Old Scotch Air

LESSON 14
The Second Position

A Capital Ship

Old English Song of the Sea

don't shift–reach back

(shift

By the Sea
Octaves in the second position

C. G.

LESSON 15
The Second Position

Theme and Variations

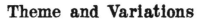

Shifting between the First and Second Positions
Extension of the fourth finger

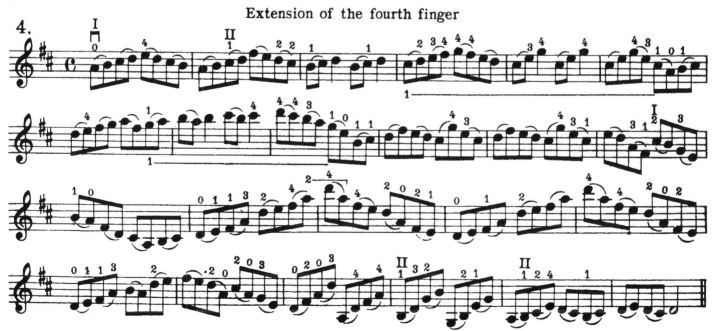

LESSON 16
Through the First, Second and Third Positions

Love Song

Study in the First, Second and Third Positions

Holy, Holy, Holy

Dykes

3. To be played in (1) the first, (2) the second, (3) the third position

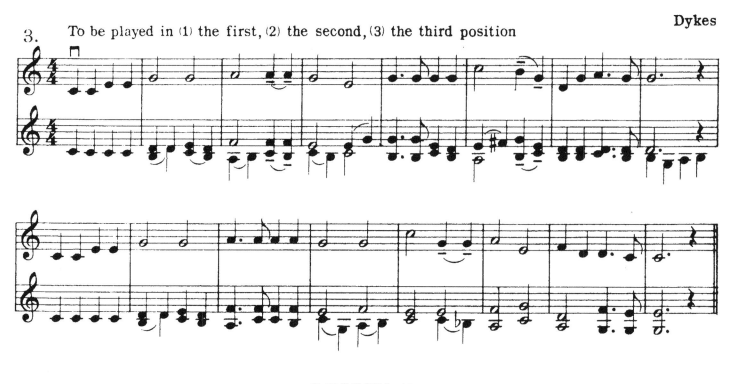

LESSON 17

Serenade

C.G.

1. Allegretto

A Study in Three Positions

Allegro Brillante

C.G.

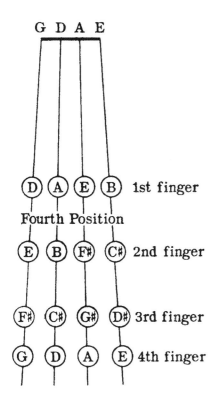

LESSON 18

The Fourth Position

Memorize the notation and fingering of the fourth position, so that the name of the note played by any finger can be recited without hesitation when called for by the teacher.

1. The hand is now held against the body of the violin.
2. The thumb is lowered, but the tip is still visible.
3. Hold the first finger down as much as possible.
4. For good intonation, check the first finger tones on the G, D, and A strings with the next open string above.

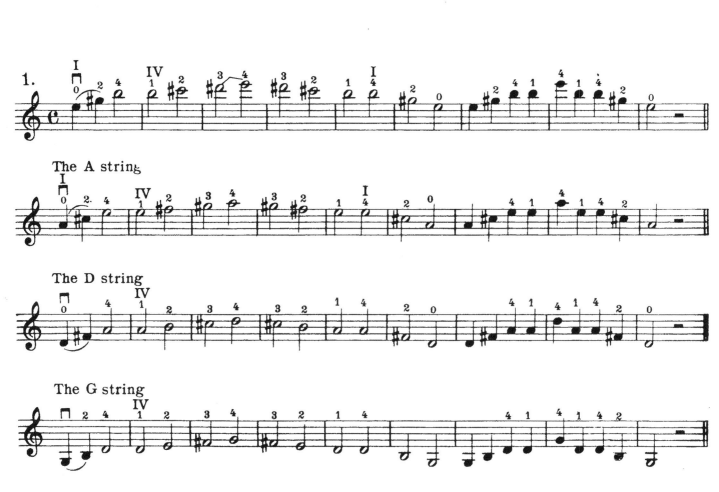

The A string

The D string

The G string

Testing with the open string above

The Winding Ayre

C.G.

Through Four Positions

LESSON 19
The Fourth Position

Play No. 3 on the A, D, and G strings

From Bygone Days

C.G.

Tempo di Gavotte

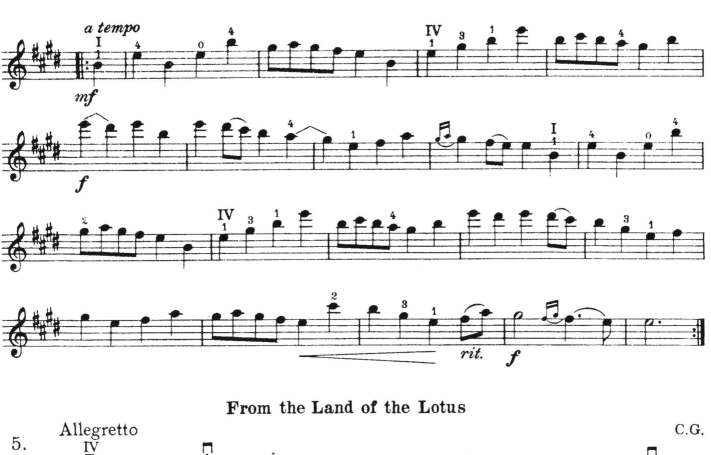

From the Land of the Lotus

C.G.

LESSON 20

The Fifth Position

Hand in the Fifth Position

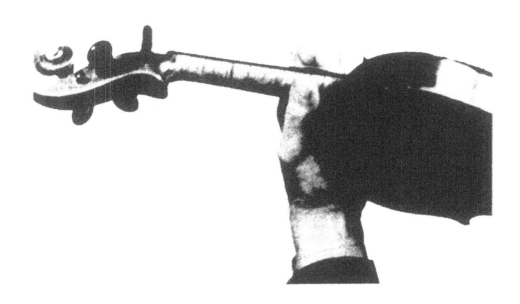

Notation and fingering of the Fifth Position

With the exception of the E string, the fingering of the fifth position is the same as the first position; i. e., the same notes with the same fingering, but on the next string below.

1. The thumb, still lower than in the fourth position, is held against the verticle base of the violin neck. The lower palm of the hand is held against the curved body of the violin.
2. Memorize the names and the fingering of the notes on the E string.
3. The half tones are much closer together than in the lower positions.

The Fifth Position

Third and Fifth Positions

Skaters Waltz

C.G.

Long, Long Ago
Play on the E, D and G strings with the same fingering

LESSON 21
The Fifth Position

Practice each shift in Nos. 2 and 3 in the first and third positions, as shown in No. 1, before making the shift to the fifth position.

Valse Galante

Autumn Shadows

C. G.

LESSON 22

The Fifth Position with typical shifts from the First and Third Positions

Trial Flight

C. G.

Au Revoir

C. G.

LESSON 23

The Sixth Position

Hand in the Sixth and Seventh Positions

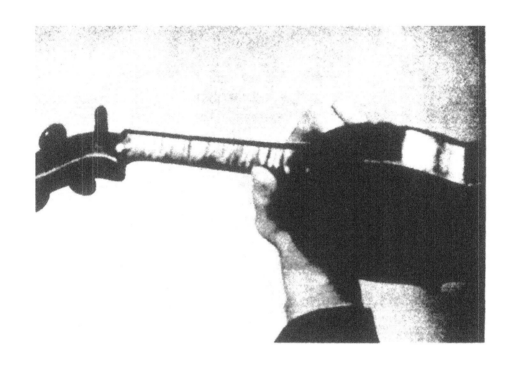

Notation and fingering of the Sixth Position

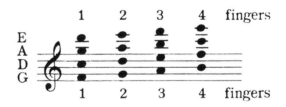

With the exception of the E string, the fingering of the sixth is the same as that of the second position.

1. The ball of the thumb contacts the curvature of the violin neck.
2. Place the first finger on its note (f) on the G string; through the semicircle thus formed, the E peg of the violin is visible to the player.
3. The left elbow must be well under the instrument.
4. Place the fingers close together for the half tones.
5. Do not raise the first finger except when crossing the strings.
6. Memorize the names and the fingering of the notes on each string.

Melody in the Sixth Position

From the second to the sixth position

Sixth Position March

LESSON 24
The Seventh Position

Notation and fingering of the Seventh Position

Using the next lower string, the fingering of the seventh is the same as that of the third position.

There is a close, technical relationalship between the second, fourth and sixth positions; likewise, there is a natural affinity between the third, fifth and seventh positions in respect to the constant shifting from one position to another.

1. Only the tip of the thumb now touches the angle of the violin neck.
2. Do not shove the fingers forward in anticipation of a change of position, the thumb, hand and fingers must move together as a coördinated unit.
3. Particularly the first finger should be kept down on the strings as much as possible.
4. The half tones in the seventh position are so close together that large fingers have to compensate slightly to play them in tune.

The Third, Fifth and Seventh Position Shifting

Each half-phrase is in the first position, then repeated an octave higher in the third, fifth and seventh positions.

Four Variations on Four Strings

LESSON 25

Thro' the Woods

Springtide